Theory Paper   Grade 4   2014   A
Model Answers

1 (a) slow (2)
       in a singing style (2)

   (b) *There are four possible answers to this question. Any of the answers shown would receive full marks.* (2)

   (c) *There are four possible answers to this question. Any of the answers shown would receive full marks.* (2)

   (d)  (4)

   (e) 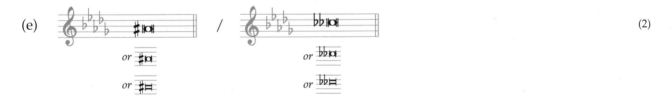 (2)

   (f)  (1)

2   *There are many ways of completing this question. Either of the specimen completions below would receive full marks.*   (10)

EITHER

   (a)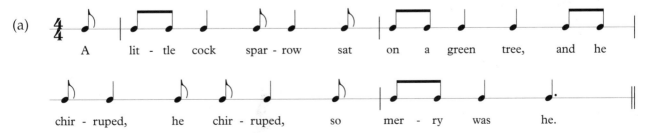

OR

(b)

3 (a) (i) enough / sufficiently (2)
animated / lively (2)
(ii) X supertonic (2)
Y subdominant (2)

(iii) (2)

(b) (i) D (2)
(ii) 16 (2)
(iii) five (2)

(iv) (4)

(c) (i) String violin / harp (2)
Woodwind flute / clarinet / oboe (2)
(ii) true (2)
false (2)
(iii) trombone / bass trombone / tuba / bass tuba (2)

4 (10)

(a)

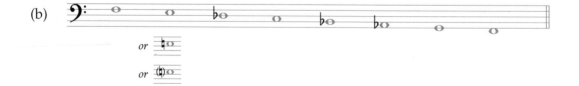

(b)

Music Theory Past Papers 2014

Model Answers

ABRSM Grade 4

Welcome to ABRSM's *Music Theory Past Papers 2014 Model Answers*, Grade 4. These answers are a useful resource for students and teachers preparing for ABRSM theory exams and should be used alongside the relevant published theory past papers.

All the answers in this booklet would receive full marks but not all possible answers have been included for practicable reasons. In these cases other reasonable alternatives may also be awarded full marks. For composition-style questions (where candidates must complete a rhythm, compose a melody based on a given opening or set text to music) only one example of the many possible answers is given.

For more information on how theory papers are marked and some general advice on taking theory exams, please refer to the Music Theory Grade 4 web page: www.abrsm.org/theory4.

Using these answers

- Answers are given in the same order and, where possible, in the same layout as in the exam papers, making it easy to match answer to question.

- Where it is necessary to show the answer on a stave, the original stave is printed in grey with the answer shown in black, for example:

- Alternative answers are separated by an oblique stroke (/) or by *or*, for example:

getting slower / gradually getting slower

- The old-style crotchet rest ⌐ is accepted as a valid alternative to the modern symbol 𝄽 .

- Answers that require the candidate to write out a scale or chord have been shown at one octave only. Reasonable alternatives at different octaves can also receive full marks.

- Sometimes the clef, key and time signature of the relevant bar(s) are included for added clarity, for example:

© 2015 by The Associated Board of the Royal Schools of Music
Published by ABRSM (Publishing) Ltd, a wholly owned subsidiary of ABRSM
Cover by Kate Benjamin & Andy Potts
Printed in England by Page Bros (Norwich) Ltd

5
1. minor 2nd (10)
2. minor 7th
3. perfect 5th
4. major 6th
5. augmented 4th

6  (10)

7 (a) (1) tonic / I (9)
     (2) subdominant / IV
     (3) dominant / V

(b)  (6)

Theory Paper   Grade 4   2014   B
Model Answers

1 (a) moderately loud / half loud / medium loud (1)

(b) dominant (2)

(c) *vite* (2)

(d) acciaccatura / grace note / crushed note (2)

(e) *There are two possible answers to this question. Either of the answers shown would receive full marks.* (2)

(f) (4)

5

(g) 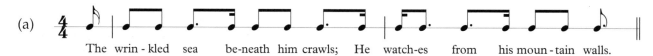 (2)

2 *There are many ways of completing this question. Either of the specimen completions below would receive full marks.* (10)

EITHER

(a)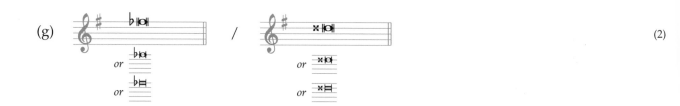

OR

(b)

3 (a) (i) with movement / with motion / moving (2)
majestic / stately (2)
prominent / make the melody stand out (2)

(ii) (2)

(iii) 12 (2)

(b) (i) (4)

(ii) B♭ (2)
(iii) G minor (2)
(iv) false (2)

(c) (i) trombone / bass trombone / tuba / bass tuba (2)
(ii)   Family   string   Instrument   violin / harp (4)
or   Family   woodwind   Instrument   flute / piccolo
or   Family   percussion   Instrument   celesta / glockenspiel / xylophone

(iii)   viola   double bass (4)

4 (10)

(a)

(b)

or

or

5   (10)

6   (10)

(a)

(b)

7   (a)   (1)   subdominant / IV   (9)
            (2)   tonic / I
            (3)   dominant / V

    (b)   B minor   B major   F minor   (6)
            dominant / V   subdominant / IV   tonic / I

Theory Paper   Grade 4   2014   C
Model Answers

1   (a)   tranquil / calm / peaceful / serene   (2)

    (b)   compound   (1)
          duple   (1)

    (c)   Similarity   rhythm / articulation   (1)
          Difference   pitch of last two notes / dynamics   (1)

    (d)   (3)

    (e)   (4)

    (f)   six   (2)

2 *There are many ways of completing this question. Either of the specimen completions below would receive full marks.* (10)

EITHER

(a)

She's the daugh-ter of the breeze, She's the dar-ling of the seas.

OR

(b)

3 (a) (i) little / a little / a bit / slightly (2)

held back / getting slower / gradually getting slower (2)

(ii) *adagio*   *largo* (4)

(iii) 16 (2)

(b) (i) G (2)

(ii) A (2)

(iii) X   diminished 5th (2)

Y   minor 2nd (2)

(iv)  (2)

(c) (i) tuba / bass tuba (2)

viola (2)

(ii) true (2)

false (2)

(iii) side drum / snare drum / bass drum / cymbals / triangle / tambourine / castanets / tam-tam (2)

4 (10)

(a)

(b)

5 (10)

(a)

(b)   trill

6 (10)

(a)

(b)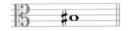

7 (a)   (1)   subdominant / IV   (9)
       (2)   dominant / V
       (3)   tonic / I

(b)    (6)

Theory Paper   Grade 4   2014   S
Model Answers

1 (a)   majestic / stately   (2)

   (b)   compound   (1)
          duple   (1)

   (c)   Similarity   rhythm / trill / grace notes   (1)
          Difference   pitch of last note   (1)

   (d) 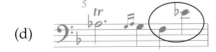   (2)

   (e) 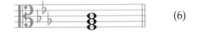   (3)

(f)   5   (2)

(g)   (2)

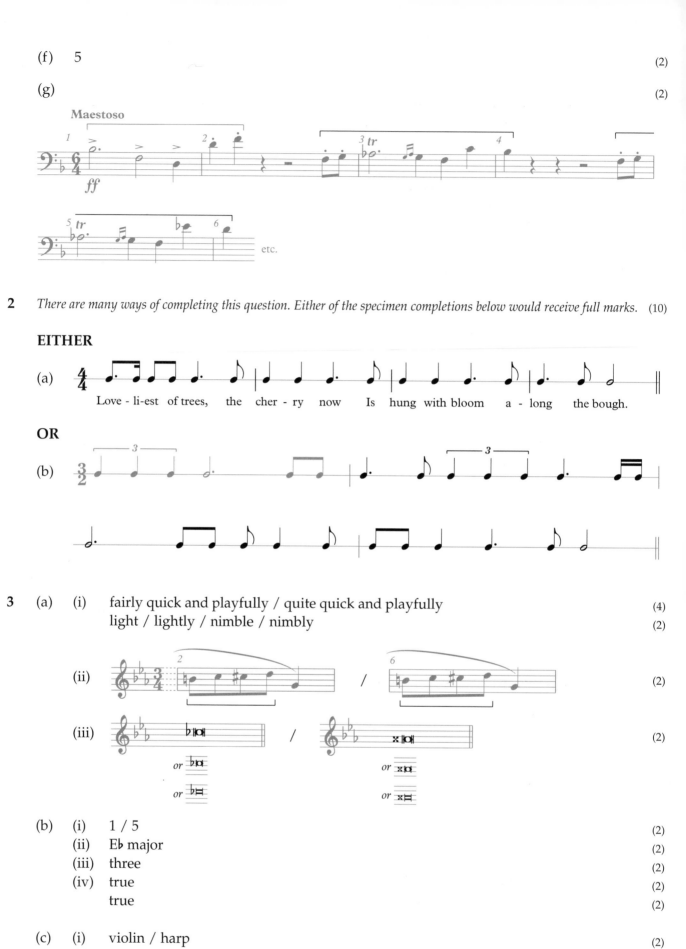

2   *There are many ways of completing this question. Either of the specimen completions below would receive full marks.*   (10)

EITHER

(a)

Love - li-est of trees,   the   cher - ry   now   Is   hung with bloom   a - long   the bough.

OR

(b)

3   (a)   (i)   fairly quick and playfully / quite quick and playfully   (4)
                   light / lightly / nimble / nimbly   (2)

      (ii)   /   (2)

      (iii)   /   (2)

            or   or

            or   or

(b)   (i)   1 / 5   (2)
      (ii)   E♭ major   (2)
      (iii)   three   (2)
      (iv)   true   (2)
             true   (2)

(c)   (i)   violin / harp   (2)
      (ii)   viola   (2)
      (iii)   flute / piccolo   (2)
      (iv)   timpani   bass drum   (4)

10

4   (10)

(a)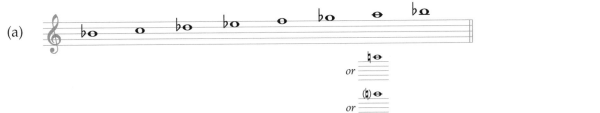

(b)

5    etc.   (10)

6   F double sharp   F flat   (10)
         G sharp   B double flat
         E flat   C sharp

7   (a)   (1)   subdominant / IV   (9)
              (2)   tonic / I
              (3)   dominant / V

(b)   (6)

Music Theory Past Papers 2014 Model Answers

Model answers for four past papers from ABRSM's 2014 Theory exams for Grade 4

Key features:

- a list of correct answers where appropriate
- a selection of likely options where the answer can be expressed in a variety of ways
- a single exemplar where a composition-style answer is required

Support material for ABRSM Theory exams

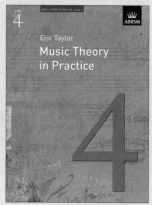

ABRSM is the exam board of the Royal Schools of Music. We are committed to actively supporting high-quality music-making, learning and development throughout the world, and to producing the best possible resources for music teachers and students.

ABRSM
24 Portland Place
London W1B 1LU
United Kingdom

www.abrsm.org

ISBN 978-1-84849-715-3

9 781848 497153

Royal Academy of Music

RCM LONDON

RNCM
ROYAL NORTHERN
COLLEGE of MUSIC

Royal Conservatoire of Scotland